GUIDE TO MONOLOGUES: WOMEN

AN INDEX OF OVER 800 MONOLOGUES FROM CLASSICAL AND MODERN PLAYS

ROBERT EMERSON
JANE GRUMBACH
EDITORS

DRAMA BOOK PUBLISHERS
NEW YORK

Library of Congress Cataloging-in-Publication Data

Guide to monologues, women.

    1. Acting—Indexes.   2. Monologues—Indexes.
3. Women—Drama—Indexes.   I. Emerson, Robert.
II. Grumbach, Jane.
PN2080.G85   1989   016.80882'45   88-33482
ISBN 0-89676-104-5

CONTENTS

Introduction. v

Classical Serious Monologues 1

Classical Comic Monologues. 4

Modern Serious Monologues 5

Modern Comic Monologues. 23

Modern Serio-Comic Monologues. 36

One Character Plays. 43

The editors wish to thank David Cleaver of Theatrebooks, 1600 Broadway, New York, New York for his invaluable assistance in preparing this book.

INTRODUCTION

This book contains monologues from published plays only. Each entry lists the title and author of the play, the character's name and age, the approximate time of performance, the first line of the speech, and the act and scene in which it appears. For modern monologues, the character's exact age is given in brackets following the name. Nationalities are given where they apply in terms of accents.

A sample entry reads:

BUS STOP	Cherie (20,	2:00	II	Bo come in one...*
William Inge	Southern)			(DPS 34)

The play is *BUS STOP* by William Inge. The speaker is Cherie, aged 20, who has a Southern accent. The approximate performance time of the monologue is two minutes. The speech appears in Act II. The first line is "Bo come in one" etc. The asterisk (*) following the first line indicates that the monologue consists of two or more speeches pieced together. (DPS 34) means that this monologue begins on page 34 of the Dramatists Play Service Acting edition. The key to abbreviations of publishers' names is listed below.

For classical monologues, line numbers are given but not specific editions, as publications of these plays are so numerous. Please note that the line numbers given here come from the Washington Square Press editions. (The Greek tradedies are the Lattimore and Green Translations; the Shakespearean plays are the Folger Library editions.) However, line numbers should vary only slightly, so locating speeches in other editions and translations should present no problem.

For modern monologues, acting editions have been used when available, although many of the plays are published in other editions. All the plays—except those published solely in acting editions—are available at bookstores and libraries all over the country.

KEY TO ABBREVIATIONS

BPP	-	Broadway Play Publishing
Dram	-	Dramatic Publishing Company
DPS	-	Dramatists Play Service
H&W	-	Hill & Wang
NAL	-	New American Library
ND	-	New Directions
Peng	-	Penguin
RH	-	Random House
S&S	-	Simon & Schuster
SF	-	Samuel French
SFL	-	Samuel French Limited
TCG	-	Theatre Communications Group

CLASSICAL SERIOUS
YOUNG

PLAY Author	Character	Run Time (approx)	Place in Text	First Line of Monologue
AGAMEMNON Aeschylus	Cassandra	2:00	I. 1256	Oh, flame and...
ANTIGONE Sophocles	Antigone	2:00	I. 891	O tomb, O marriage...
ELECTRA Euripides	Electra	2:00	I. 112	Quicken the foot's rush...
ELECTRA Euripides	Electra	1:30	I. 299	I will tell if I must...
ELECTRA Sophocles	Electra	1:30	I. 87	O Holy Light...
ELECTRA Sophocles	Electra	2:30	I. 254	Women I am ashamed...
ELECTRA Sophocles	Electra	1:30	I. 341	It is strange indeed...
ELECTRA Sophocles	Electra	2:00	I. 431	My dear one, not a morsel...
ELECTRA Sophocles	Electra	2:30	I. 558	I will tell you...
HENRY IV Part 1 Shakespeare	Lady Percy	1:00	II iii 38	O my good lord, why are...
IPHIGENIA IN AULIS Euripides	Iphigenia	3:00	I. 1211	O my father, if I had...
IPHIGENIA IN AULIS Euripides	Iphigenia	2:00	I. 1278	O pitiable am I...
IPHIGENIA IN AULIS Euripides	Iphigenia	3:00	I. 1367	Mother, now listen to my words...

THE LIBATION BEARERS Aeschylus	Electra	1:30	I. 183	The bitter wash has surged...
MEDEA Euripides	Medea	2:00	I. 214	Women of Corinth, I have come...
MEDEA Euripides	Medea	2:30	I. 365	Things have gone badly...
MEDEA Euripides	Medea	2:30	I. 465	O coward in every way...
MEDEA Euripides	Medea	2:30	I. 764	God, and God's daughter...
MEDEA Euripides	Medea	2:00	I. 869	Jason, I beg you to be...
MEDEA Euripides	Medea	3:00	I. 1021	O children, O my children...
THE MERCHANT OF VENICE—Shakespeare	Portia	1:00	III ii 42	Away then! I am locked...
THE MERCHANT OF VENICE—Shakespeare	Portia	1:00	IV i 189	The quality of mercy is not strained...
ORESTES Euripides	Electra	4:00	I. 1	There is no form of anguish...
ORESTES Euripides	Electra	2:30	I. 959	O country of Pelasgia...
PROMETHEUS BOUND Aeschylus	Io	2:00	I. 640	I know not how I should...
RICHARD III Shakespeare	Lady Anne	1:30	I ii 1	Set down, set down your honorable load...
ROMEO AND JULIET Shakespeare	Juliet	1:00	II ii 90	Thou knowest the mask...
ROMEO AND JULIET Shakespeare	Juliet	1:15	III ii 1	Gallop apace, you fiery- footed steeds...
ROMEO AND JULIET Shakespeare	Juliet	1:45	IV iii 15	Farewell! God knows when...

THE TROJAN WOMEN Euripides	Cassandra	1:30	I. 308	Lift up, heave up; carry the flame...
THE TROJAN WOMEN Euripides	Cassandra	3:00	I. 353	O mother, star my hair with flowers...
THE TROJAN WOMEN Euripides	Andromache	3:00	I. 634	O mother, our mother, hear me...
THE TROJAN WOMEN Euripides	Andromache	2:30	I. 740	O darling child I loved too well...
THE TROJAN WOMEN Euripides	Helen	2:30	I. 914	Perhaps it will make no difference...
THE WINTER'S TALE Shakespeare	Hermione	1:30	III ii 23	Since what I am to say must be but...
THE WINTER'S TALE Shakespeare	Paulina	1:15	III ii 193	What studied torments, tyrant...

MIDDLE AGED

AGAMEMNON Aeschylus	Clytemnestra	3:00	I. 855	Grave gentlemen of Argolis...
ANTHONY AND *CLEOPATRA* Shakespeare	Cleopatra	1:00	IV xv 88	No more but e'en a woman...
ELECTRA Euripides	Clytemnestra	2:00	I. 1011	And dark and lonely were your father's...
ELECTRA Sophocles	Clytemnestra	1:30	I. 516	It seems your are loose...
ELECTRA Sophocles	Clytemnestra	1:00	I. 636	Phoebus Protector, hear me...
HENRY IV Part 2 Shakespeare	Lady Percy	1:45	II iii 10	O yet, for God's sake...
HENRY VIII Shakespeare	Queen Katherine	1:45	II iv 15	Sir, I desire you do me right...
IPHIGENIA IN AULIS Euripides	Clytemnestra	1:30	I. 899	Oh, you were born of a goddess...

IPHIGENIA IN AULIS Euripides	Clytemnestra	3:30	I. 1147	Hear me now...
MACBETH Shakespeare	Lady Macbeth	1:30	I v 1	They met me in the day...

OLD

CORIOLANUS Shakespeare	Volumnia	3:30	V iii 147	Nay, go not from us thus.
RICHARD III Shakespeare	Queen Margaret	1:45	IV iv 92	I called thee then...
THE TROJAN WOMEN Euripides	Hecuba	2:00	I. 98	Rise, stricken head, from the dust...
THE TROJAN WOMEN Euripides	Hecuba	2:00	I. 466	No. Let me lie where I have fallen.
THE TROJAN WOMEN Euripides	Hecuba	3:00	I. 969	First, to defend the honor of the gods...
THE TROJAN WOMEN Euripides	Hecuba	2:00	I. 1156	Lay down the circled shield...

CLASSICAL - COMIC
YOUNG

AS YOU LIKE IT Shakespeare	Rosalind	1:15	III v 39	And why, I pray you?
AS YOU LIKE IT Shakespeare	Rosalind	1:45	V ii 28	O, I know where you are!
THE LEARNED WOMEN Moliere	Armande	1:00	I i 26	Lord, what a sordid mind your words...
LOVE'S LABORS LOST Shakespeare	Princess	1:00	V 11889	A time, methinks, too short...
A MIDSUMMER NIGHT'S DREAM—Shakespeare	Helena	1:00	I i 232	How happy some o'er other...
A MIDSUMMER NIGHT'S DREAM—Shakespeare	Titiania	2:00	II i 65	Then I must be thy lady...*

THE MISANTHROPE Moliere	Celimene	2:00	III iv913	Madame, do not misjudge my attitude...
MUCH ADO ABOUT *NOTHING*—Shakespeare	Hero	1:30	III i 51	O god of love!*
SCAPIN Moliere	Zerbinette	3:00	III iii	This has nothing to do with you...*
THE SCHOOL FOR WIVES Moliere	Agnes	2:00	II v	It's the most amazing story...*
THE TAMING OF THE *SHREW*—Shakespeare	Katherine	2:00	V ii 158	Fie, fie! Unknit that...
TWELFTH NIGHT Shakespeare	Viola	1:00	II ii 17	What means this lady?
THE WAY OF THE WORLD Congreve	Mrs. Millamant	1:45	IV i	My dear liberty, shall I leave...*

MODERN SERIOUS
AGE UNDER 20

ANGIE'S SONG—Ruth Jacobson in "Glimpses"	Angie (young)	2:00	1-act	I guess I've always been... (Dram 85)
DOES A TIGER WEAR A *NECKTIE?* Don Petersen	Linda (18, Black)	1:15	I, 2	When I was born...* (DPS 39)
EASTER August Strindberg in "Three Plays"	Eleonora (16)	1:00	II	Do you know what I... (Peng 157)
EDEN Steve Carter	Annetta (18, West Indian)	1:00	III	Papa, what can I... (SF 85)
ELEEMOSYNARY Lee Blessing	Echo (16)	1:45	sc. 7	Uncle Bill hardly remem- bers...* (DPS 46)
FRESH HORSES Larry Ketron	Jewel (16, Southern)	1:30	II	He knew it was some body... (DPS 55)
IN WHITE AMERICA Martin Duberman	Girl (15, Black)	2:45	II	The night before I was so excited...* (SF 62)

JOURNEY TO THE DAY Roger O. Hirson	Katherine (19)	1:30	II, 2	He needed us... (DPS 52)
LEMON SKY Lanford Wilson	Carol (17)	1:15	I	Oh, Ronnie, would you...* (DPS 25)
LILY DALE Horton Foote	Lily (18)	1:15	II, 3	Oh, Brother. Brother! (DPS 56)
LIVING AT HOME Anthony Giardina	Mary (19)	2:15	I, 2	I guess I must... (DPS 27)
THE LOVE SUICIDE AT SCHOFIELD BARRACKS Romulus Linney	Miss Borden (19)	2:00	II	His wife asked me over...* (DPS 45)
LOVERS (WINNERS) Brian Friel	Mag (17, Irish)	1:30	ep. 1	Everything's so still. (Dram 36)
OF POEMS, YOUTH, AND SPRING John Logan	Susan (16)	1:00	sc. 3	Yes, today. Things are... (SF 17)
THE PASSION OF JOSEF D. Paddy Chayefsky	Nadya (17)	1:15	I, 1	Volinsky soldiers! Three hundred...* (SF 6)
REQUIEM FOR BROTHER X—William Mackey in "Black Drama Anthology"	Bonita (teen- aged, Black)	1:15	1- act	Yes siree, Daddy. (NAL 333)
RESPONSIBLE PARTIES Jeffrey Sweet	Tina (18)	1:15	sc. 2	My Dad never gave me...* (DPS 45)
RITES Caroline White	Wendy (18)	4:00	1-act	My name is Wendy. (Dram 39)
A SEA OF WHITE HORSES Peter Dee	Janice (18)	2:00	I	I'm still trying to... (SF 36)
THE STRAW Eugene O'Neill in "Six Short Plays"	Eileen (18)	1:45	II, 2	Then I want to say... (RH 96)
TO GILLIAN ON HER 37TH BIRTHDAY Michael Brady	Rachel (16)	1:15	II, 2	This was my mother's...* (BPP 46)

WINTERSET Maxwell Anderson	Miriamne (15)	1:00	III	Mio—I'd have gone...* (DPS 88)

AGES 20 - 30

THE ADVERTISEMENT Natalia Ginzburg in "Plays By & About Women"	Teresa (20's)	4:00	I	He found us in bed together. (RH 318)
THE ADVERTISEMENT Natalia Ginzburg in "Plays By & About Women"	Teresa (20's)	1:30	III	I could have married... (RH 343)
AGNES OF GOD John Pielmeier	Agnes (21)	1:15	II, 4	Why are you crying? (SF 73)
ALL GOD'S CHILLUN GOT WINGS—Eugene O'Neill in "Nine Plays"	Ella (20's)	1:45	II, 1	It's his Old Man... (RH 120)
AMADEUS Peter Shaffer	Costanze (20's)	1:00	II	Hush now, lovey.* (SF 108)
ANDROCLES AND THE LION—Bernard Shaw	Lavinia (20's)	1:30	I	That is the strange thing, Captain... (Peng 121)
ANNA CHRISTIE Eugene O'Neill	Anna (20, Swedish)	1:00	III	I s'pose I tried... (RH 134)
ANNE OF THE THOUSAND DAYS—Maxwell Anderson	Anne (20, English)	2:00	II,7	I've never thought what it... (DPS 71)
AUNT DAN AND LEMON Wallace Shawn	Lemon (25, English	5:00	1-act	Hello, dear audience... (DPS 11)
THE BALCONY Jean Genet	Carmen (20's)	1:15	sc. 5	Excuse me.* (Grove 37)
BALM IN GILEAD Lanford Wilson	Ann (20's)	1:30	II	Like the devil gets... (H&W 63)
BAR & GER Geraldine Aron	Ger (20's South African)	2:15	1-act	My heart has been... (SF 16)
A BEAST STORY Adrienne Kennedy	Beast Girl (20's, Black)	1:00	1-act	My father comes to the door... (SF 36)

BIRDBATH Leonard Melfi in "Encounters"	Velma (26)	1:45	1-act	NOOOOOOOO! YOU STAY AWAY...* (SF 39)
BLOOD MOON Nicholas Kazan	Manya (mid- 20's)	1:30	I	Hello. My name is... (SF 5)
BLUES FOR MISTER *CHARLIE*—James Baldwin	Juanita (20, Black)	2:30	III	He lay beside me on that bed... (SF 112)
CHILDREN OF DARKNESS Edwin Justus Mayer	Laetitia (29)	1:00	III	Do you think you...* (SF 86)
COME ON STRONG Garson Kanin	Ginny (20's)	3:30	I,3	Let me tell you...* (DPS 30)
A COMPANY OF *WAYWARD SAINTS* George Herman	Isabella (20's)	1:45	II	I haven't been very honest...* (SF 102)
CONFESSIONS OF A *FEMALE DISORDER* Susan Miller in "Gay Plays"	Coop (late 20's)	1:00	I, 6	All right. I'll... (Avon 154)
DAYS OF WINE AND *ROSES*—J. P. Miller	Kirsten (25)	1:15	I	I dreamed one time...* (DPS 12)
DON JUAN Moliere	Elvira (20's)	3:00	IV	Don't be surprised...* (DPS 41)
ECHOES N. Richard Nash	Tilda (20's)	1:30	II	Now listen to me... (SF 51)
EDUCATING RITA Willy Russell	Rita (27, English)	1:30	I, 7	I'm all right with...* (SF 31)
THE ENTERTAINER John Osborne	Jean (22, English)	1:30	sc. 3	Well, it's—oh it's a complicated... (Dram 26)
EX-MISS COPPER QUEEN *ON A SET OF PILLS* Megan Terry	Copper Queen (26)	1:30	1-act	Hey there, Mister... (SF 51)
EXTREMITIES William Mastrosimone	Marjorie (20's)	1:15	I, 3	Police. Charges. (SF 33)
FUNNYHOUSE OF A *NEGRO*—Adrienne Kennedy	Negro (20)	2:30	1-act	Part of the time I live with Raymond... (SF 7)

GETTIN' IT TOGETHER Richard Wesley	Coretta (23, Black)	1:15	sc. 2	All I ever been... (DPS 33)
THE GINGHAM DOG Lanford Wilson	Gloria (27, Black)	3:00	II	I used to notice windows. (DPS 52)
THE GINGHAM DOG Lanford Wilson	Gloria (27, Black)	1:45	I	I used to pray, I really... (DPS 41)
GOLD Eugene O'Neill in "Six Short Plays"	Sue (20)	1:30	II	It's something between Pa... (RH 147)
THE GOOD WOMAN OF *SETZUAN* Bertolt Brecht	Shen Te (20's)	1:00	sc. 5	Something terrible has happened. (Grove 89)
HAVING WONDERFUL *TIME*—Arthur Kober	Teddy (20)	1:15	III, 2	I've stood just about... (DPS 80)
IS THERE LIFE AFTER *HIGHSCHOOL?* Jeffrey Kindley	Roxanne (28)	1:15	I	What I remember most... (SF 27)
JUDITH Jean Giraudoux	Judith (20's, Israeli)	1:30	II	Is it you, is it Daria? (DPS 43)
JUNEBUG GRADUATES *TONIGHT*—Archie Shepp in "Black Drama Anthology"	Sonja (20, Black)	1:15	II, 1	I'm thinkin' I'd like... (NAL 64)
KEY EXCHANGE Kevin Wade	Lisa (Late 20's)	1:00	sc. 3	When I was very young... (DPS 18)
LADY WINDERMERE'S *FAN*—Oscar Wilde in "Plays"	Lady Winder- mere (21, English)	1:30	III	Why doesn't he come? (Peng 45)
LITTLE MOON OF ALBAN James Costigan	Brigid Mary (20, Irish)	1:30	I	A year. A whole year... (SF 40)
LOOK BACK IN ANGER John Osborne	Alison (25, English)	1:30	II, 1	Why? there must be...* (Dram 36)
LOOK BACK IN ANGER John Osborne	Alison (25, English)	1:00	III, 2	It doesn't matter. I was wrong... (Dram 78)
LOOK HOMEWARD, ANGEL Ketti Frings	Laura (23)	1:30	III	Mrs. Gant, this isn't easy. (SF 80)

LUDLOW FAIR Lanford Wilson in "Balm in Gilead and Other Plays"	Rachel (mid- 20's)	1:30	1-act	There's nothing wrong... (H&W 76)
LUDLOW FAIR Lanford Wilson in "Balm in Gilead and Other Plays:	Agnes (25)	3:30	1-act	Well sleep it off. (H&W 89)
MADEMOISELLE *COLOMBE* Jean Anouilh	Colombe (20's)	1:00	II,1	An anonymous letter... (SF 61)
MARAT/SADE Peter Weiss	Corday (24)	1:15	sc. 29	In my room in Caen...* (Dram 97)
MASTERPIECES Arthur Bicknell	Charlotte (20's)	1:15	II	Oh, Bran... (DPS 58)
MECCA Ted Whitehead	Sandy (20, English)	3:00	II, 2	It all happened so...* (Faber 76)
MIDDLE OF THE NIGHT Paddy Chayefsky	The Girl (24)	2:00	I, 3	It just burst out of me.* (SF 21)
MISS JULIE August Strindberg in "Strindberg: 5 Plays"	Julie (25)	1:30	1-act	No, I don't want... (NAL 95)
A MOON FOR THE *MISBEGOTTEN* Eugene O'Neill	Josie (28, Irish-American)	1:15	III	That's right. (SF 92)
MUSEUM Tina Howe	Tink (20's)	3:00	1-act	At least once...* (SF 52)
MY LIFE Corinne Jacker	Sally (20's)	2:15	II	I used to be... (DPS 37)
1918 Horton Foote	Elizabeth (24, Texan)	2:15	sc. 2	Bessie, don't. (DPS 47)
ODODO Joseph A. Walker in "Black Drama Anthology"	Actress M (20's, Black)	1:15	II	Of course all black... (NAL 362)
PYGMALION Bernard Shaw	Liza (20, English)	1:30	V	Oh, you are a cruel...* (Peng 108)

RING ROUND THE MOON—Jean Anouilh	Isabelle (20's)	1:45	III, 1	Well, are you satisfied... (DPS 63)
THE RIVER NIGER Joseph A. Walker	Ann (22, Black)	1:30	I	Quietly. Ma takes everything...* (SF 24)
THE RIVER NIGER Joseph A. Walker	Gail (21, Black)	1:15	II	If you really know... (SF 54)
SALOME Oscar Wilde	Salome (20's)	3:30	1-act	There is no sound. (Peng 345)
THE SEA GULL Anton Chekhov	Nina (20's)	2:30	IV	Why do you say you kiss the ground...* (SF 59)
THE SIGN IN SIDNEY BRUSTEIN'S WINDOW Lorraine Hansberry	Iris (29)	1:15	I, 2	You don't know what it's like... (SF 45)
THE SILVER CORD Sidney Howard	Christina (20's)	3:00	II, 2	Have you ever thought...* (SF 69)
SPARKS FLY UPWARD Lawrence & Lee	Felicia (20's)	1:45	II, 5	God and I talk...* (DPS 79)
STAR OF THE MORNING Loften Mitchell in "Black Drama Anthology"	Lottie (20's, Black)	3:00	II, 7	You have to go nowhere.* (NAL 636)
STRANGE INTERLUDE Eugene O'Neill in "Three Plays"	Nina (21)	2:30	Part 1, Act III	It's a queer house. (RH 98)
STRANGE INTERLUDE Eugene O'Neill in "Three Plays"	Nina (23)	2:30	Part 1, Act V	There! That can't be my imagination... (RH 132)
STREET SCENE Elmer Rice	Rose (20)	1:45	III	I like you so much, Sam.* (SF 233)
SWEET BIRD OF YOUTH Tennessee Williams	Heavenly (20's, Southern)	3:00	II	If you're going to...* (DPS 47)
TAKE A GIANT STEP Louis Peterson	Christine (Late 20's, Black)	1:30	II, 2	My father was killed in the mills...* (SF 72)
TAKEN IN MARRIAGE Thomas Babe	Annie (20's)	1:00	II	You are so lonely...* (DPS 45)

TELL ME THAT YOU LOVE ME, JUNIE MOON D.D. Brooke	Junie (20)	1:45	I	He wasn't much... (Dram 19)
THE THREE SISTERS Anton Chekhov	Marsha (20's)	1:30	III	I want to confess... (SF 78)
U.S.A. Dos Passos & Shyre	Player F (Any age)	5:00	II	In San Francisco in 1878... (SF 63)
UNCLE VANYA Anton Chekhov	Elena (27)	2:00	III	There is nothing worse... (SF 37)
VALENTINE'S DAY Horton Foote	Elizabeth (21, Texan)	1:30	sc. 3	When I was three... (DPS 37)
THE VIGIL Ladislas Fodor	Magdalen (Late 20's)	2:30	II	But I was barren.* (SF 79)
A VOICE OF MY OWN Elinor Jones	Mary Shelley (20's)	1:15	1-act	November, 1815. Dream that... (DPS 22)
THE WISDOM OF EVE Orr & Denham	Eve (20's)	3:00	I	I'm afraid it's...* (DPS 20)
A WOMAN OF NO IMPORTANCE—Oscar Wilde in "Plays"	Hester (20's)	1:00	II	Lord Henry Watson.* (Peng 103)
WOMEN OF MANHATTAN John Patrick Shanley	Rhonda (28, Southern)	2:30	sc. 1	I know what you think...* (DPS 12)
THE WOOLGATHERER William Mastrosimone	Rose (20's)	1:45	I	You may think it's... (SF 28)
A YARD OF SUN Christopher Fry	Ana-Clara (20's)	1:30	I	As an article of... (Dram 38)

AGES 30 - 40

AND A NIGHTINGALE SANG—C.P. Taylor	Helen (30's, English)	1:45	II, 2	On the next morning...* (Dram 85)
BAD SEED Maxwell Anderson	Mrs. Daigle (30's)	2:00	I, 4	Rest. Sleep. When you...* (DPS 34)
THE BEACH HOUSE Nancy Donohue	Annie (37)	1:15	III, 1	Well, I tell you... (SF 62)

BEST FRIEND Michael Sawyer	Carolyn (Late 30's)	5:00	II	Oh, honey, come...* (SF 58)	
BETWEEN TWO THIEVES Warner LeRoy	Blonde (30)	1:30	II	No, I'm not an... (SF 56)	
BLUE WINDOW Craig Lucas	Libby (33)	3:00	sc. 3	I didn't know a soul...* (SF 62)	
BRIGHTON BEACH MEMOIRS—Neil Simon	Blanche (38)	1:15	II	...I'm not going to... (SF 95)	
CAMILLE Alexandre Dumas	Marguerite (30's)	2:00	I, 2	Why? Do you want... (SF 68)	
CANADIAN GOTHIC Joanna M. Glass	Jean (30, Canadian)	1:15	1-act	I've looked for him... (DPS 23)	
CAT ON A HOT TIN ROOF Tennessee Williams	Margaret (30, Southern)	2:00	I	I know, believe me, I know that... (DPS 27)	
A CLEARING IN THE WOODS—Arthur Laurents	Virginia (30's)	1:30	I	Eight days ago, I went... (DPS 15)	
CRAIG'S WIFE George Kelly	Mrs. Craig (30's)	1:00	II	Well, what if I have... (SF 91)	
DANNY & THE DEEP BLUE SEA John Patrick Shanley	Roberta (31)	1:15	sc. 3	I made my father...* (DPS 36)	
A DAY IN THE DEATH OF JOE EGG—Peter Nichols	Sheila (35, English)	3:00	I	I join in these jokes to please him. (SF 28)	
A DAY IN THE DEATH OF JOE EGG—Peter Nichols	Sheila (35, English)	1:30	I	One of these days I'll hit him. (SF 14)	
THE DAY THEY SHOT JOHN LENNON James McLure	Fran (35)	1:30	1-act	There's a very melan choly... (DPS 29)	
THE DEATH OF A MINER Paula Cizmar	Mary Alice (32)	1:45	I	You see, one day... (SF 63)	
DESIRE UNDER THE ELMS—Eugene O'Neill in "Three Plays"	Abbie (35)	1:30	I, 4	If cussin' me does... (RH 21)	

DUEL OF ANGELS Jean Giraudoux	Lucile (30)	1:15	I	You must forgive me... (DPS 26)
FATHER'S DAY Oliver Hailey	Estelle (30's)	1:15	II	I admire Marian... (DPS 60)
FITS AND STARTS Grace McKeaney in "Chicks"	Babs (30's)	1:45	1-act	I'd run over... (SF 76)
FOOL FOR LOVE Sam Shepard	May (Early 30's)	3:30	1-act	You want me to finish...* (DPS 36)
HELLO AND GOODBYE Athol Fugard	Hester (30's, White South African)	1:45	I	Not like that. Maybe frightened... (SF 13)
HELLO AND GOODBYE Athol Fugard	Hester (30's, White South African)	1:00	II	They pushed me... (SF 46)
THE JEWISH WIFE Bertold Brecht	The Wife (36, Jewish)	3:30	1-act	Yes, I'm going now, Fritz. (Grove 13)
LADIES IN WAITING Peter De Anda in "Black Drama Anthology"	Carmen (30, Black)	1:15	II, 1	Shee! My last... (NAL 503)
LADIES IN WAITING Peter De Anda in "Black Drama Anthology"	Agrippa (30, Black)	2:30	II, 3	I wanted the chair... (NAL 521)
LADY WINDERMERE'S FAN—Oscar Wilde in "Plays"	Mrs. Erlynne (30's, English)	2:00	III	Believe what you choose... (Peng 49)
LANDSCAPE OF THE BODY—John Guare	Betty (30's)	1:45	II	It bothered me... (DPS 55)
LATER Corinne Jacker	Kate (30's)	1:45	II	I can sail... (DPS 37)
LEAR Edward Bond	Bodice (30's)	1:15	II, 4	War. Power. (Dram 56)
LITTLE VICTORIES Lavonne Mueller	Joan (30's)	1:15	I	Let me tell you...* (DPS 27)
LOSING TIME John Hopkins	Joanne (30's)	3:00	I	Well, I knew a guy... (BPP 23)

LOU GEHRIG DID NOT DIE OF CANCER—Jason Miller in "Three One-Act Plays"	Mrs. Martin (30's)	1:00	1-act	But, you see, I had... (DPS 41)
THE MAIDS Jean Genet	Solange (30's)	7:00	1-act	Madame...At last! (Grove 91)
MECCA Ted Whitehead	Jill (38, English)	1:15	II, 1	They smile at you... (Faber 65)
MORE STATELY MANSIONS Eugene O'Neill	Sara (30's, Irish)	1:45	III, 2	God help me... (Yale 190)
'NIGHT, MOTHER Marsha Norman	Jessie (Late 30's)	1:00	1-act	I found an old baby picture... (DPS 50)
NO EXIT Jean-Paul Sartre	Estelle (30's)	2:00	1-act	Hah! Mine? All right, which one... (SF 37)
NUTS Tom Topor	Claudia (Early 30's)	2:30	III	Wait a second...* (SF 83)
ORPHEUS DESCENDING Tennessee Williams	Carol (30's, Southern)	1:30	I, 2	I used to be what they call... (DPS 19)
THE PETRIFIED FOREST Robert Sherwood	Mrs. Chisholm (35)	1:15	II	You haven't the remotest... (DPS 60)
PORCH Jeffrey Sweet	Amy (30)	1:30	1-act	My father's daughter. (SF 34)
RECKLESS Craig Lucas	Rachel (30's)	2:00	sc. 27	I'm here. (DPS 54)
ROOTS IN A PARCHED GROUND—Horton Foote	Julia (32)	2:00	1-act	No, I didn't see them. (DPS 38)
THE RUFFIAN ON THE STAIR—Joe Orton in "Complete Plays"	Joyce (30's, English)	2:00	sc. 3	I can't go to the park. (Grove 39)
THE SEA HORSE Edward J. Moore	Gertrude (Late 30's)	1:30	II	I was sitting... (SF 51)
THE SIGN IN SIDNEY BRUSTEIN'S WINDOW Lorraine Hansberry	Mavis (30's)	2:15	II, 3	You know, sometimes... (SF 95)

SNOWANGEL—Lewis John Carlino in "Cages"	Connie (30's)	1:30	1-act	He came to me while I was... (DPS 24)
STRANGE INTERLUDE Eugene O'Neill in "Three Plays"	Nina (35)	1:00	Part 2, Act 7	No longer my baby... (RH 171)
A STREETCAR NAMED DESIRE Tennessee Williams	Blanche (30's, Southern)	1:30	I, 1	I, I, I took the blows... (DPS 16)
A STREETCAR NAMED DESIRE Tennessee Williams	Blanche (30's, Southern)	1:45	II, 2	He was a boy, just a boy... (DPS 67)
THE STY OF THE BLIND PIG—Phillip Hayes Dean	Alberta (30's, Black)	1:30	II, 2	Then I had to read... (DPS 51)
TALK TO ME LIKE THE RAIN AND LET ME LISTEN—Tennessee Williams in "27 Wagons Full of Cotton"	Woman (30's)	4:30	1-act	I will receive a check... (ND 216)
TIME LIMIT! Henry Denker & Ralph Berkey	Mrs. Cargill (30's)	2:30	II	You know a man... (SF 42)
TO BE YOUNG, GIFTED AND BLACK Robert Nemiroff	First Actress (30's, Black)	1:45	II, 1	April 27, 1962. Dear Kenneth... (SF 71)
TO GILLIAN ON HER 37TH BIRTHDAY Michael Brady	Gillian (37)	1:15	II, 4	Oh, you're not listening... (BPP 57)
TONIGHT WE IMPROVISE Luigi Pirandello	Mommina (30)	6:00	III	Here it is! (SF 92)
TWINKLE, TWINKLE Ernest Thompson in "Answers"	Andrea (33)	1:30	1-act	Screw women's liberation! (DPS 67)
UNCLE VANYA Anton Chekhov	Sonia (30)	1:45	IV	What can we do... (SF 61)
A WEEKEND NEAR MADISON Kathleen Tolan	*Nessa (Early* 30's)	1:15	sc. 1	So what if there... (SF 24)

THE WHITE WHORE AND THE BIT PLAYER Tom Eyen in "Ten Plays"	The Nun (30's)	1:30	1-act	Put away, dear! (SF 322)
WINE IN THE WILDERNESS Alice Childress	Tommy (30's, Black)	1:30	1-act	I don't stay mad...* (DPS 37)
THE WINSLOW BOY Terence Rattigan	Catherine (30, English)	1:00	II, 2	Sir Robert finished... (DPS 76)
THE WISDOM OF EVE Mary Orr & Reginald Denham	Karen (30's)	4:00	III	The day following Eve's... (DPS 70)
A WOMAN OF NO IMPORTANCE—Oscar Wilde in "Plays"	Mrs. Arbuthnot (38, English)	1:30	III	Gerald, come near to me. (Peng 126)

AGES 40 - 60

THE ADDING MACHINE Elmer Rice	Mrs. Zero (45)	5:30	sc. 1	I gettin' sick o' them Westerns. (SF 1)
AGNES OF GOD John Pielmeier	Dr. (40's)	1:30	I, 6	Oh, we would get... (SF 29)
AGNES OF GOD John Pielmeier	Mother (Middle-aged)	1:00	I, 10	When I was a... (SF 48)
AMERICAN DREAMS Studs Terkel (Adapt—Frisch)	Romona (40's, American Indian)	4:00	I	I'm a member of the... (DPS 29)
AND THINGS THAT GO BUMP IN THE NIGHT Terrance McNally	Ruby (50)	1:45	III	We will continue. (DPS 89)
THE BASIC TRAINING OF PAVLO HUMMEL David Rabe	Mrs. Hummel (50's)	4:00	II	In Stratford, Connecticut... (SF 61)
BODIES James Saunders	Helen (Middle-aged, English)	1:30	II	You cling to that... (DPS 53)
BOESMAN AND LENA Athol Fugard	Lena (50's, Black)	1:45	I	All you knew was... (SF 9)

CAMINO REAL Tennessee Williams	Marguerite (40's)	1:30	Block10	Oh, Jacques, we're used to each other... (DPS 63)
CHAMBER MUSIC Arthur Kopit in "The Day the Whores Come Out to Play Tennis..."	Woman in Aviatrix's Outfit (40's)	1:00	1-act	All right, check the records... (H&W 12)
THE CHERRY ORCHARD Anton Chekhov	Lyuboff (40's)	2:00	III	What truth? You see where the... (SF 59)
DANCING IN THE *ENDZONE*—Bill C. Davis	Madeleine (Middle-aged)	1:30	II	Yes. I know... (SF 74)
DEAR LIAR Jerome Kilty	Mrs. Campbell (40's, English)	1:15	II	There! It is just this... (SF 39)
DEAR LOVE Jerome Kilty	Elizabeth (40, English)	2:30	I	Mr. Browning, I am accustomed... (SF 21)
DUET FOR ONE Tom Kempinski	Stephanie (Middle-aged)	3:30	ses. 3	Well—I suppose... (SF 21)
EQUUS Peter Shaffer	Dora (40's, English)	2:30	sc. 23	Look, Doctor... (SF 69)
EXIT THE KING Eugene Ionesco	Marguerite (40)	2:30	1-act	He can still distinguish colors. (Grove 93)
FENCES August Wilson	Rose (43, Black)	2:00	II, 5	You can't be nobody... (NAL 97)
FIVE FINGER EXERCISE Peter Shaffer	Louise (40's, English)	2:30	I, 2	I'm not a very...* (SF 27)
THE GINGERBREAD LADY Neil Simon	Toby (Early 40's)	1:00	III	You're not twenty-two... (SF 68)
THE GLASS MENAGERIE Tennessee Williams	Amanda (50, Southern)	1:30	I, 2	I went straight... (DPS 16)
THE GRASS HARP Truman Capote	Dolly (50)	1:45	I, 1	Once...once when... (DPS 19)
HALLOWEEN Leonard Melfi in "Encounters	Margaret (50)	1:00	1-act	Don't be smart, young man. (SF 86)

INADMISSIBLE EVIDENCE John Osborne	Mrs. Garnsey (40's, English)	1:30	I	I don't know.* (Dram 74)
JOHNNY NO-TRUMP Mary Mercier	Florence (43)	1:15	II	I don't know how to... (DPS 56)
THE KILLING OF SISTER GEORGE—Frank Marcus in "Gay Plays"	Mercy (40's, English)	1:30	III	Stop Crying. (Avon 410)
LADYHOUSE BLUES Kevin O'Morrison	Liz (41)	2:00	I	That girl ain't...* (SF 44)
A LATE SNOW Jane Chambers in "Gay Plays"	Margo (40's)	1:15	II	I was married...* (Avon 325)
A LESSON FROM ALOES Athol Fugard	Gladys (40's, South African)	1:30	II	Please...please...I prom- ised...(SF 65)
LITTLE FEARS Emanuel Peluso	Older Woman (Middle-aged)	3:00	1-act	Will you be late? (DPS 12)
LONG DAY'S JOURNEY INTO NIGHT Eugene O'Neill	Mary (54, Irish-American)	2:30	III	It kills the pain. (Yale 104)
LONG DAY'S JOURNEY INTO NIGHT Eugene O'Neill	Mary (54, Irish-American)	2:30	III	No, dear. But I... (Yale 114)
LONG DAY'S JOURNEY INTO NIGHT Eugene O'Neill	Mary (54, Irish-American)	1:15	IV	I had a talk with... (Yale 175)
LOOK AWAY Jerome Kilty	Mary (56)	3:00	I	Doctors, you say... (SF 7)
LOOK AWAY Jerome Kilty	Elizabeth (Middle-aged, Black)	3:00	I	Elizabeth Keckley...* (SF 9)
LOOK HOMEWARD,ANGEL Ketti Frings	Eliza (57)	1:45	III	Well, I'll deposit the money...* (SF 89)
A MEDAL FOR WILLIE William Branch in "Black Drama Anthology"	Mrs. Jackson (40's, Black)	4:30	sc. 7	Why? All right... (NAL 470)

MOMMA'S LITTLE *ANGELS*—Louis LaRusso II	Patsie (40's)	1:30	I, 2	When I think... (DPS 18)
MORE STATELY *MANSIONS* Eugene O'Neill	Deborah (50's)	5:00	III, 2	God, how long have... (Yale 162)
MOURNING BECOMES *ELECTRA*—Eugene O'Neill in "3 Plays"	Christine (40)	1:30	"The Hunted" I, 1	Vinnie, I—I must... (RH 289)
MOURNING BECOMES *ELECTRA*--Eugene O'Neill in "3 Plays"	Christine (40)	2:00	"The Hunted" II	Well, you can go... (RH 301)
THE MUTILATED Tennessee Williams	Trinket (50)	2:00	sc. 2	Such a clear, frosty night... (DPS 20)
NEVIS MOUNTAIN DEW Steve Carter	Zepora (45, Black)	1:30	II	Ayton, think back! (DPS 33)
OUT OF OUR FATHER'S *HOUSE*—Eve Merriam	Mary (50's)	1:30	1-act	I went to Kensington... (SF 34)
PIAF Pam Gems	Piaf (40's)	1:15	II, 6	You heard. Florence...* (SF 61)
PORTRAIT OF A *MADONNA*—Tennessee Williams in "27 Wagons Full of Cotton"	Miss Collins (Middle-aged, Southern)	2:30	I	I left my parasol once... (ND 99)
THE RIVER NIGER Joseph A. Walker	Mattie (50's, Black)	1:30	II	In heaven! Treasures in heaven! (SF 39)
THE ROSE TATTOO Tennessee Williams	Serafina (Early 40's, Italian)	1:00	I, 5	I count up the nights... (DPS 33)
SATURDAY, SUNDAY, *MONDAY* Eduardo de Filippo	Rosa (50's, Italian)	2:15	II	Giuliane, come here. (SF 74)
THE SHADOW BOX Michael Cristofer	Agnes (Middle-aged)	2:00	II	You see, it was...* (SF 59)
THE SHADOW BOX Michael Cristofer	Beverly (Middle-aged)	1:45	II	Let me tell you...* (SF 71)

THE SHADOW BOX Michael Cristofer	Maggie (40)	1:30	II	For Christ's sake...* (SF 77)
THE SILVER CORD Sidney Howard	Mrs. Phelps (50's)	2:30	III	I was twenty... (SF 89)
THE SLAVE LeRoi Jones	Grace (40)	1:30	1-act	What? Is no one to... (Morrow 67)
SMALL CRAFT WARNINGS Tennessee Williams	Leona (Middle-aged)	1:30	II	My time's run out... (ND 70)
STEVIE Hugh Whitemore	Stevie (Middle- aged, English)	2:00	I	It's like escaping... (SFL 20)
THE SUBJECT WAS ROSES Frank D. Gilroy	Nettie (45)	2:00	II, 3	I think it was his energy... (SF 64)
SUMMERTREE Ron Cowen	Mother (40's)	1:30	II	You know, when it comes... (DPS 29)
SWEET BIRD OF YOUTH Tennessee Williams	Princess (Middle-aged)	1:30	III	Why did I give him the number? (DPS 55)
TOE JAM Elaine Jackson in "Black Drama Anthology"	Mother (50's, Black)	1:15	II, 2	Xenith, I worked... (NAL 662)
A TOUCH OF THE POET Eugene O'Neill	Deborah (41)	2:00	II	It is natural you should admire that... (Yale 82)
A TOUCH OF THE POET Eugene O'Neill	Nora (40, Irish)	2:30	IV	Ah, it's you, darlin'! (Yale 136)
WELCOME TO ANDROMEDA—Roy Whyte	Nurse (40's)	1:45	1-act	He took two knitting... (SF 37)
WHO'S AFRAID OF VIRGINIA WOOLF? Edward Albee	Martha (45)	2:15	III	Hey, hey...Where is... (DPS 86)
THE WISDOM OF EVE Mary Orr & Reginald Denham	Margo (45)	1:15	III	Karen started this story... (DPS 103)
ZOOMAN & THE SIGN Charles Fuller	Rachel (Middle-aged, Black)	1:45	II	What is it... (SF 33)

ALL OVER Edward Albee	Wife (71)	1:30	II	It's very different. (SF 61)
ANASTASIA Marcelle Maurette	Empress (70's, Russian)	1:00	II	Malenkaia! Malenkaia! (SF 64)
BOSOMS & NEGLECT John Guare	Henny (83)	3:00	II	James? James? (DPS 61)
CHILDREN A.R. Gurney, Jr.	Mother (60's)	3:30	II	Pokey? Pokey. (DPS 51)
CONTRIBUTION Ted Shine in "Contributions"	Mrs. Love (70, Black)	1:15	1-act	And it put your daddy...* (DPS 56)
A DAY IN THE DEATH *OF JOE EGG*—Peter Nichols	Grace (65, English)	2:00	II	No, well I wouldn't have... (SF 46)
THE ENTERTAINER John Osborne	Phoebe (60, English)	2:15	sc. 6	You don't know what it's like.* (Dram 49)
FLIGHT LINES Barbara Schneider	Christie (60's)	5:00	sc. 4	I've been watching you. (DPS 26)
THE LAST OF MRS. *LINCOLN*—James Prideaux	Mary (60)	3:15	II, 5	My dearest Lewis. (DPS 58)
THE LOVES OF CASS *MCGUIRE*—Brian Friel	Cass (70, Irish)	1:15	II	Hi, I made damn sure... (SF 30)
THE MAN IN THE GLASS *BOOTH*—Robert Shaw	Old Woman (German)	2:30	II	I have sat and sat. (SF 55)
THE ROOM Harold Pinter in "Complete Works: One"	Rose (60, English	3:45	1-act	Here you are. This'll keep the cold out. (Grove 101)
THE STY OF THE BLIND *PIG*--Phillip Hayes Dean	Weedy (70's, Black)	1:15	I, 4	Just because I'm... (DPS 23)
SUNRISE AT *CAMPOBELLO*—Dore Schary	Sara (60's)	1:15	II, 2	I wonder if you... (DPS 64)
TAKEN IN MARRIAGE Thomas Babe	Ruth (60's)	2:45	I	I may seem the... (DPS 19)

WATERCOLOR Philip Magdalany	Diane (Old)	1:30	1-act	You're lying. I know it. (DPS 47)

MODERN COMIC
AGE UNDER 20

BUTTERFLIES ARE FREE Leonard Gershe	Jill (19)	1:00	I, 2	I guess it was right... (SF 34)
CINDERS Janusz Glowacki	Prince (16)	1:15	sc. 7	I'm in here for... (SF 54)
COURTSHIP Horton Foote	Laura (17, Texan)	1:15	1-act	Everything bad that...* (DPS 39)
COYOTE UGLY Lynn Siefert	Scarlet (12)	1:30	sc. 9	I blame my whole... (DPS 34)
THE EFFECTS OF GAMMA RAYS ON MAN-IN-THE-MOON MARIGOLDS Paul Zindel	Janice (16)	1:15	II, 2	The Past. I got the cat... (DPS 39)
FEIFFER'S PEOPLE Jules Feiffer	Little Girl	1:15		So, I was standing on the corner... (DPS 77)
GOD'S SPIES Don Nigro	Wendy (19)	4:00	1-act	And I asked my mama...* (SF 8)
HAPPY BIRTHDAY, WANDA JUNE Kurt Vonnegut, Jr.	Wanda June (8)	1:15	I, 4	Hello. I am Wanda June. (SF 24)
INNOCENT THOUGHTS, HARMLESS INTENTIONS John Heuer	The Girl (18)	1:15	II	Item! Flash! Item! (DPS 34)
LOVERS (WINNERS) Brian Friel	Mag (17, Irish)	1:45	episode1	I can see the boarders... (Dram 23)
THE LUCKY SPOT Beth Henley	Cassidy (15, Southern)	2:30	II, 2	Look here, my knees...* (DPS 47)
THE MEMBER OF THE WEDDING Carson McCullers	Frankie (12, Southern)	1:15	II	Boyoman! Manoboy!* (ND 87)

ONCE UPON A PLAYGROUND Jack Frakes	Dixie (13)	1:00	1-act	I don't know why...* (SF 13)
RALLY ROUND THE FLAG, BOYS! David Rogers	Comfort (16)	1:15	I, 1	Dear Elvis, I suppose you're... (Dram 18)
THE REAL THING Tom Stoppard	Debbie (17, English)	1:30	II, 3	What, *House of Cards?** (SF 74)
SLOW DANCE ON THE KILLING GROUND William Hanley	Rosie (18)	2:15	II, 1	If you knew me better... (DPS 41)
SNOW LEOPARDS Martin Jones	Sally (18, W. Virginian)	1:00	II	People think I sound...* (SF 42)
TABLE SETTINGS James Lapine	Grand-daughter (14)	1:15	1-act	Stephen Franklin and... (SF 63)
THINKING PINK Ruth Jacobson in "Glimpses"	Girl (Young)	2:30	1-act	I'm here to talk... (Dram 50)
TITANIC Christopher Durang	Lidia (18)	1:45	sc. 1	I'm the Captain's...* (DPS 15)
WHAT I DID LAST SUMMER—A.R. Gurney, Jr.	*Bonny (14)*	*1:15*	*II*	*You know what this...* (DPS 52)

AGES 20 - 30

ACCOMODATIONS Nick Hall	Pat (Early 20's)	1:15	II, 1	You know, I think... (SF 28)
AFTER HAGGERTY David Mercer	Claire (Late 20's)	2:30	II, 5	Don't say it, Haggerty! (Methuen 72)
AGATHA SUE, I LOVE YOU Abe Einhorn	Agatha (20's)	1:00	I, 2	I'll bet you're going... (SF 30)
AMERICAN DREAMS Studs Terkel—Adapt Frisch	Emma (20)	4:00	I	It's mostly what's known... (DPS 38)
THE BALD SOPRANO Eugene Ionesco in "4 Plays"	Mary (20's)	1:15	1-act	Elizabeth and Donald are now... (Grove 19)
BLUES FOR MISTER CHARLIE—James Baldwin	Jo (20's)	1:15	III	Am I going to spend the rest... (SF 99)

BORN YESTERDAY Garson Kanin	Billie (20's)	1:00	II	I got this letter today.* (DPS 50)
BUS STOP William Inge	Cherie (20, Southern)	2:00	II	Bo come in one...* (DPS 34)
CHOCOLATE CAKE Mary Gallagher in "Win/Lose/Draw"	Annmarie (20's)	2:30	1-act	Well...I...I put... (DPS 48)
COSTAL DISTURBANCES Tina Howe	Holly (24)	1:15	I, 5	If you dissect a...* (SF 54)
COFFEE A RELATIVITY Herbert Hartig & Lois Balk in "The Best of Broadway"	Pretty Girl (Young)	1:45	I	"Another cup of... (Dram 46)
THE COLORED MUSEUM George C. Wolfe	Miss Pat (20's, Black)	5:00	1-act	Welcome aboard Celeb- rity...* (BPP 1)
DREAM GIRL Elmer Rice	Georgina (23)	3:00	I	If I could only stop... (DPS 13)
FEIFFER'S PEOPLE Jules Feiffer	Young Girl (20)	1:00		Try to see it my way. (DPS 41)
THE FOREIGNER Larry Shue	Catherine (20's, Southern)	3:30	I, 2	Mind if I sit... (DPS 41)
GETTING OUT Marsha Norman	Arlie (20's)	2:45	II	No. I don't have to... (DPS 42)
THE HARVESTING John Bishop	Louise (20's, Black)	1:15	II	Christ, what a rotten...* (DPS 45)
HERE LIES JEREMY *TROY*—Jack Sharkey	Kathryn (Late 20's)	1:00	II	All this time. (SF 66)
THE HIGH AND THE *FLIGHTY*—Arnold Rosen & Coleman Jacoby in "The Best of Broadway"	Hostess (20's)	1:15	II	There's absolutely no cause...* (Dram 78)
HOOTERS Ted Tally	Cheryl (25)	1:15	II, 6	Hey, Clint. (DPS 64)
AN IDEAL HUSBAND Oscar Wilde in "Plays"	Mrs. Cheveley (27, English)	1:30	I	My dear Sir Robert... (Peng 170)

AN IDEAL HUSBAND Oscar Wilde in "Plays"	Mabel (25, English)	1:15	II	Well, Tommy has proposed... (Peng 192)
THE IMPORTANCE OF *BEING EARNEST* Oscar Wilde in "Plays"	Gwendolen (20's, English)	1:15	II	Oh! It is strange he...* (Peng 291)
IN THE BOOM BOOM *ROOM*—David Rabe	Susan (20's)	1:30	I	All through my sopho- more... (SF 39)
IN WHITE AMERICA Martin Duberman	Eliza (20's, Southern)	1:30	II	Washington, Georgia. No power... (SF 39)
IS THERE LIFE AFTER *HIGH SCHOOL?* Jeffrey Kindley	Ellen (28)	1:00	I	I don't want to... (SF 12)
JUMPERS Tom Stoppard	Dotty (Late 20's, English)	1:30	I	And yet, Professor... (Grove 35)
JUMPERS Tom Stoppard	Dotty (Late 20's, English)	1:15	II	Well, it's all... (Grove 74)
KENNEDY'S CHILDREN Robert Patrick	Rona (29)	1:00	I	I hate this bar. (SF 8)
LITTLE MURDERS Jules Feiffer	Patsy (27)	2:30	II, 1	Screaming! You son of a bitch...* (SF 42)
LUNCH HOUR Jean Kerr	Carrie (23)	1:00	I	Actually, just before...* (SF 22)
LUNCHTIME Leonard Melfi in "Encounters"	Avis (25)	1:30	1-act	When I first met George... (SF 66)
MESSIAH Martin Sherman	Rachel (28)	1:30	II	Dear God, I never... (Amber Lane 35)
MISS LONELYHEARTS Howard Teichmann	Betty (20's)	1:15	I, 4	God only knows about men... (DPS 24)
A MONTH IN THE *COUNTRY*--Ivan Turgenev	Natalia (29)	1:00	II, 1	He does not love her! (SF 71)
NEXT TIME I'LL SING *TO YOU*—James Saunders	Lizzie (20's)	3:00	II	I suppose so. Not that I'm... (DPS 40)

NOON—Terence McNally in "Morning, Noon and Night"	Allegra (Early 20's)	2:45	1-act	Bonjour! Bonjour! (SF 65)
OH, MEN! OH, WOMEN! Edward Chodorov	Mildred (20's)	7:30	I	Well—I awakened Miss Tacher...* (SF 31)
THE OWL AND THE PUSSYCAT--Bill Manhoff	Doris (26)	1:00	I	You know I once wrote...* (SF 25)
PERIOD OF ADJUSTMENT Tennessee Williams	Isabel (20's, Southern)	2:00	I	I'm so wound up...* (DPS 11)
THE PUBLIC EYE Peter Shaffer	Belinda (22, English)	2:30	1-act	All right...First let me tell you...* (SF 32)
ROMANOFF AND JULIET Peter Ustinov	Juliet (20's)	1:30	II	Oh, why must the mind... (DPS 35)
SEXUAL PERVERSITY IN CHICAGO—David Mamet	Joan (20's)	1:00	1-act	What are you doing? (SF 33)
SHERLOCK'S LAST CASE Charles Marowitz	Lisa (20's)	1:45	I, 2	What you never knew...* (DPS 20)
SHIVAREE William Mastrosimone	Shivaree (20's)	2:15	I	Well, sport, you can... (SF 33)
THE SKIN OF OUR TEETH Thornton Wilder	Sabina (Early 20's)	3:00	I	Oh, oh, oh! Six o'clock... (SF 10)
SLEEPING BEAUTY Laurence Klavan	Louise (28)	1:00	1-act	I'm twenty-eight... (DPS 14)
SOAP OPERA Ralph Pape in "Girls We Have Known..."	Lucy (Mid-20's)	1:45	1-act	For the first few... (DPS 59)
SOLOMON'S CHILD Tom Dulack	Naomi (21)	1:15	I	I know your son... (DPS 29)
A SONG TO FORGET Arnold Auerbach in "The Best of Broadway"	Miss Twitchell (Young)	1:30	I	Gee, it was a wonderful...* (Dram 13)
THE STAR-SPANGLED GIRL—Neil Simon	Sophie (23, Southern)	1:30	I, 2	Mr. Cornell, ah have tried... (DPS 20)

THE STAR-SPANGLED GIRL--Neil Simon	Sophie (23, Southern)	1:15	I, 2	Two years ago in Japan... (DPS 23)
TABLE SETTINGS James Lapine	Girl-friend (Late 20's)	2:30	1-act	Some people never... (SF 51)
THIRD & OAK: THE LAUNDROMAT Marsha Norman	Deedee (20's)	1:30	1-act	I don't want to start... (DPS 21)
TIMES SQUARE Leonard Melfi in "Encounters"	Marigold (Early 20's)	2:45	1-act	My name is Marigold...* (SF 172)
TIMES SQUARE Leonard Melfi in "Encounters"	Laura Jean (Early 20's, Southern)	1:30	1-act	I want you to kiss me... (SF 178)
TIRA TELLS EVERY-THING THERE IS TO KNOW ABOUT HERSELF Michael Weller	Tira (20)	2:00	1-act	Yes, I know... (DPS 26)
TRIBUTE Bernard Slade	Sally (Early 20's)	1:00	II, 1	Hi! Whenever I... (SF 53)
THE TYPISTS Murray Schisgal	Sylvia (20's)	1:15	1-act	My family never had money problems. (DPS 12)
UNCOMMON WOMEN & OTHERS Wendy Wasserstein	Muffet (27)	3:00	I, 4	I am so tired. (DPS 20)
WHERE HAS TOMMY FLOWERS GONE? Terrence McNally	Nedda (20's)	1:45	II	I'd like to ask Tommy... (DPS 46)
XMAS IN LAS VEGAS Jack Richardson	Emily (Late 20's)	1:45	I, 2	Lionel, you remind me...* (DPS 9)
YANKS 3 DETROIT 0 TOP OF THE SEVENTH Jonathan Reynolds	Donna (20's)	1:15	1-act	Duke first came to... (DPS 63)

AGES 30 - 40

AND MISS REARDON DRINKS A LITTLE Paul Zindel	Anna (30's)	2:00	II	I was teaching at Jefferson...* (DPS 24)

THE ART OF DINING Tina Howe	Elizabeth (Early 30's)	1:30	II, 2	In fact, when I... (SF 52)
BETWEEN DAYLIGHT *AND BOONVILLE* Matt Williams	Marlene (Mid-30's)	1:45	I	This one time... (SF 35)
COLORED PEOPLE'S TIME Leslie Lee	Nadine (30's, Black)	1:00	I	Yeah, I got me... (SF 48)
CUBA SI Terrence McNally	Cuba (30's, Cuban)	1:30	1-act	Bastard. Dirty hooligan... (DPS 7)
DOMINO COURTS William Hauptman	Flo (30's)	1:45	1-act	See, it's not the food...* (SF 48)
FATHER'S DAY Oliver Hailey	Louise (30's)	1:00	I	Marian, I'm going to...* (DPS 17)
FEIFFER'S PEOPLE Jules Feiffer	Miss Sacrosanct (30's)	1:30		Hello, is this Mr. Mergendeiler? (DPS 57)
A GIRL'S GUIDE TO *CHAOS*—Cynthia Heimel	Cynthia (30's)	3:00	1-act	One night I was sitting... (S&S 71)
HAPPY ENDING Douglas T. Ward	Ellie (Late 30's, Black)	1:15	1-act	I cook the food, scrub the floor... (DPS 17)
HOLD ME! Jules Feiffer	Woman (30's)	1:00	I	I talk too much. (DPS 6)
HOLD ME! Jules Feiffer	Virgin (30's)	1:00	I	Monday: I met... (DPS 13)
THE HOUSE OF BLUE *LEAVES*—John Guare	Bunny (30's)	1:15	I	I'm not that kind... (SF 15)
HUNTING COCKROACHES Janusz Glowacki	She (30's, Polish)	3:00	I	My name is Anka. (SF 8)
HURLYBURLY David Rabe	Bonnie (30's)	2:45	II	Drugs. I mean, I'm...* (SF 91)
THE ICEMAN COMETH Eugene O'Neill	Cora (30's)	1:15	I	No, dis round's on me. (RH 73)
IT HAD TO BE YOU Taylor & Bologna	Theda (30's)	3:15	I	My quality?... (SF 9)

JESSE & THE BANDIT QUEEN—David Freeman	Belle (30)	1:15	I	I regard myself... (SF 5)
KENNEDY'S CHILDREN Robert Patrick	Carla (30's)	2:00	I	I threw myself... (SF 22)
KINGDOM OF EARTH Tennessee Williams	Myrtle (30, Southern)	5:00	sc. 1	Lie down, baby...* (DPS 30)
THE LADY AND THE CLARINET Michael Cristofer	Luba (30's)	1:45	1-act	I didn't hear from... (DPS 34)
LANDSCAPE OF THE BODY—John Guare	Rosalie (30's)	2:00	I	Honeybunch, I get this...* (DPS 20)
LES LIAISONS DANGEREUSES Christopher Hampton	Merteuil (30's)	2:15	I, 4	Well, as a matter...* (SF 36)
LOVE IN A PUB Fredi Towbin in "24 Hours PM"	Linda (30's)	2:15	1-act	The aborigines are really... (DPS 47)
LUV Murray Schisgal	Ellen (30's)	1:15	II	You talk about misery!* (DPS 47)
MARCO POLO SINGS A SOLO—John Guare	Diane (30's)	2:00	I	I really started... (DPS 29)
MARY, MARY Jean Kerr	Mary (30's)	1:15	II	Bob, you won't believe this... (DPS 60)
MOLLY AND JAMES Sheila Walsh	Molly (Early 30's)	3:00	1-act	I have enough to... (SF 69)
NIGHT AND DAY Tom Stoppard	Ruth (30's, English)	2:00	II	Of course I loved him...* (SF 65)
THE NINETY-DAY MISTRESS--J.J. Coyle	Phyllis (30)	1:00	II, 3	Well...you know me... (SF 72)
NOT ENOUGH ROPE Elaine May	Edith (25-35)	1:45	1-act	Look, I lied about the rope. (SF 13)
OBJECTIVE CASE Lewis John Carlino	She (30)	1:30	1-act	Allow me to introduce myself. (DPS 40)

PAINTING CHURCHES Tina Howe	Mags (Early 30's)	2:30	I, 2	Remember how you...* (SF 36)
THE PRIMARY ENGLISH CLASS—Israel Horovitz	Wastba (30)	2:00	I	Hi, I'm Ms... (DPS 24)
THE PRIME OF MISS JEAN BRODIE Jay Allen	Brodie (35, English)	2:00	I, 2	Little girls. I am in the business... (SF 7)
THE PRISONER OF SECOND AVENUE Neil Simon	Edna (30's)	3:00	II, 1	Mel? Mel, I'm home. (SF 32)
ROSE Andrew Davies	Rose (30's, English)	1:30	II	Why did I have to... (SF 60)
RUBBERS Jonathan Reynolds	Mrs. Brimmins (38)	1:45	1-act	Thank you, Mr... (DPS 21)
SALLY AND MARSHA Sybille Pearson	Marsha (30)	1:30	I, 2	Let me tell you...* (DPS 15)
SCUBA DUBA Bruce Jay Friedman	Jean (Early 30's)	1:45	II	Harold, will you just listen...* (DPS 40)
SEASON'S GREETINGS Alan Ayckbourn	Rachel (38, English)	1:30	I, 3	I just wanted to... (SFL 47)
SPECIAL OCCASIONS Bernard Slade	Amy (39)	2:00	I, 4	My name is Amy... (SF 38)
STUFFINGS James Prideaux	Gladys (30's)	1:30	1-act	Excuse me a moment... (DPS 17)
TABLE SETTINGS James Lapine	Wife (30's)	1:30	1-act	I've always been happy. (DPS 33)
TAKEN IN MARRIAGE Thomas Babe	Dixie (Late 30's)	3:00	I	I was really...* (DPS 24)
TAKEN IN MARRIAGE Thomas Babe	Andy (Early 30's)	1:00	II	Nobody came to... (DPS 29)
THIS BIRD OF DAWNING SINGETH ALL NIGHT LONG Phillip Hayes Dean	Nancy (35, Black)	1:15	1-act	Yes, ma'am, dey sho is... (DPS 16)

TIES Jeffrey Sweet	Carol (30's)	1:15	I	My ex-husband called...* (DPS 41)
TRIBUTE Bernard Slade	Hilary (30's)	1:45	I	Okay, maybe it's... (SF 28)
WATCH THE BIRDIE Norman Krasna	Gladys (30)	1:30	I, 4	Oh, I'm in love...* (DPS 28)
WHAT WOULD JEANNE *MOREAU DO?*—Elinor Jones	Cathy (Late 30's)	5:00	1-act	I am the only person... (SF 38)
WHERE HAS TOMMY *FLOWERS GONE?* Terrence McNally	Tommy's old flame (30's)	1:15	II	Hi, Tommy. Remember me? (DPS 44)
A WOMAN OF NO *IMPORTANCE*--Oscar Wilde in "Plays"	Mrs. Allonby (30's, English)	1:15	II	He should persistently... (Peng 100)
THE WOMEN Clare Boothe Luce	Olga (30's)	1:00	I, 2	Yeah. It was a couple... (DPS 19)

AGES 40 - 60

AN ALMOST PERFECT *PERSON*--Judith Ross	Irene (40's)	2:15	Prologue	My friends, three... (SF 5)
ANY WEDNESDAY Muriel Resnik	Dorothy (40)	1:45	II, 2	Brilliant! I couldn't be... (DPS 63)
THE AUTOGRAPH HOUND James Prideaux	Lila (40's)	1:30	sc. 1	She said that one night...* (DPS 32)
BEYOND THERAPY Christopher Durang	Charlotte (Middle-aged)	1:45	I, 3	Uh, life is so difficult...* (SF 21)
CHEATERS Michael Jacobs	Grace (40's)	1:45	I, 2	I was remembering... (SF 15)
CINDERELLA WALTZ Don Nigro	Mother Magee (Middle-aged, Texan)	1:00	sc. 3	Hi, Gang. How's... (SF 61)
COME BLOW YOUR *HORN*—Neil Simon	Mother (50's, Jewish)	2:15	II	Hello? Who? (SF 44)

CONTINENTAL DIVIDE Oliver Hailey	Mae (40's)	1:15	I, 1	Trash. Mr. John carries...* (DPS 18)
COUNTING THE WAYS Edward Albee	She (50)	2:00	sc. 15	Look here! (DPS 24)
A COUPLA WHITE *CHICKS SITTING* *AROUND TALKING* John Ford Noonan	Hannah Mae (40's, Texan)	1:15	II, 1	Carl Joe arrives on...* (SF 31)
DEATH COMES TO US *ALL, MARY AGNES* Christopher Durang	Vivien (45)	3:00	sc. 2	Dear Diary, I have... (DPS 50)
THE DRAPES COME Charles Dizenzo	Mrs. Fiers (Middle-aged)	1:30	1-act	I'm faster than a...* (DPS 14)
DUCKS AND LOVERS Murray Schisgal	Mrs. Hathaway (40's)	1:15	I, 2	I won't beat about...* (DPS 22)
GEMINI Albert Innaurato	Bunny (40)	1:45	I, 1	That bitch, Mary...* (DPS 15)
GERTRUDE STEIN & *A COMPANION* Win Wells	Gertrude (Late 50's)	1:45	II	Damn them. Damn them. (SF 29)
THE GNADIGES *FRAULEIN* Tennessee Williams	Molly (40, Southern)	2:30	1-act	WHY!—He regarded her... (DPS 30)
GOLDA William Gibson	Golda (40's)	2:15	I	I have no speech. (SF 44)
GOODBYE FREDDY Elizabeth Diggs	Nessa (40)	1:45	II, 1	Look—men insisted that... (DPS 41)
GREATER TUNA J. Williams et al.	Vera (Middle- aged)	2:00	II	Oh—Hiii. Vera Carp. (SF 46)
HOTEL PARADISO Feydeau & Desvallieres	Angelique (Middle-aged)	1:30	III	Well, as you know...* (SF 101)
THE HOUSE OF BLUE *LEAVES*—John Guare	Bananas (45)	1:45	I	My troubles all began... (SF 31)
INVITATION TO A MARCH Arthur Laurents	Camilla (40's)	1:45	III	Sit down and shut up! (DPS 65)

LADY WINDERMERE'S FAN—Oscar Wilde in "Plays" English)	Duchess (40's,	2:00	I	Ah, what indeed, dear?* (Peng 20)
LAST OF THE RED HOT LOVERS—Neil Simon	Jeanette (40)	1:30	III	Do you know Charlotte Korman...* (SF 65)
LOVERS AND OTHER STRANGERS Taylor & Bologna	Bea (45-55)	1:15	4	And Joan, of all the pictures... (SF 40)
LOVERS AND OTHER STRANGERS Taylor & Bologna	Bea (45-55)	1:30	4	Well, here it is...* (SF 42)
MARCO POLO SINGS A SOLO—John Guare	Mrs. McBride (50's)	10:00	I	As I was saying... (DPS 22)
THE METEOR Friedrich Durrenmatt	Frau Nomsen (50's)	2:00	II	Nomsen. My father...* (Dram 64)
THE MUTILATED Tennessee Williams	Trinket (50)	1:15	sc. 1	Celeste, we're through... (DPS 11)
NUNSENSE (Musical) Dan Goggin	Rev. Mother (Middle-aged)	2:00	I	I tell ya, it's not... (SF 38)
THE OCTETTE BRIDGE CLUB—P.J. Barry	Connie (56)	1:15	II, 1	The other day I was... (SF 56)
OH DAD, POOR DAD, MAMMA'S HUNG YOU IN THE CLOSET AND I'M FEELIN' SO SAD Arthur Kopit	Madame Rose-pettle (40's)	10:00	sc.3	Now you don't really want to leave...* (SF 39)
THE PERFECT PARTY A.R. Gurney, Jr.	Sally (40's)	1:00	II	Oh God, this party. (DPS 34)
PLAZA SUITE Neil Simon	Norma (Middle-aged)	1:30	III	Hello?...Hello, operator? (SF 71)
RAVENSWOOD Terrence McNally in "Bad Habits"	Dolly (50's)	2:15	1-act	Not all tropical... (DPS 19)
SCENES FROM AMERICAN LIFE A.R. Gurney, Jr.	Woman (40's)	1:15	I	Um. I want to make... (SF 32)

THE SHOW-OFF George Kelly	Mrs. Fisher (50's)	2:30	I	...but she might... (SF 6)
A SLIGHT ACHE Harold Pinter in "Complete Works: One"	Flora (Middle- aged, English)	4:00	1-act	I shall wave from the window... (Grove 190)
SUGAR BABIES (Musical) Ralph Allen	Hortense (40's)	3:00	I, 15	My name is Hortense... (SF 62)
WHERE HAS TOMMY FLOWER'S GONE? Terrence McNally	Tommy's Mother (50's)	1:15	I	Your father and I... (DPS 14)
WHERE IS DE QUEEN? Jean-Claude Van Itallie in "War and Four Other Plays"	Nanny (Middle-aged)	1:15	1-act	Excuse me. Excuse me. (DPS 64)
WINTER CHICKEN Jennifer Jarrett	Eleanor (47)	1:15	I, 1	Before I dial... (DPS 11)

AGE OVER 60

AND I AIN'T FINISHED YET--Eve Merriam	Moms (Old, Black)	7:00	1-act	Howdy, children. (SF 43)
HOLD ME! Jules Feiffer	Miss Baum (60's)	2:45	I	Hello God. (DPS 24)
LEGENDS! James Kirkwood	Leatrice (60)	1:15	II, 2	Umm, my last play... (SF 74)
THE MADWOMAN OF CHAILLOT Jean Giraudoux	Countess (70)	4:00	I	To be alive is to...* (DPS 26)
PHOTO FINISH Peter Ustinov	Stella (Old)	2:15	I	Now...no...yes... (DPS 5)
ROSE Andrew Davies	Mother (60's, English)	1:15	II	You know I was wear- ing...* (SF 48)
THE STY OF THE BLIND PIG Phillip Hayes Dean	Weedy (70, Black)	1:45	II, 1	We sure would have... (DPS 36)

AND THINGS THAT GO BUMP IN THE NIGHT Terrence McNally	Lakme (13)	1:45	II	Thirteen! Thirteen years... (DPS 49)
BRIGHTON BEACH MEMOIRS—Neil Simon	Nora (16)	1:30	I	Oh, God, he was...* (SF 21)
THE COLORED MUSEUM George C. Wolfe	Normal (Teens, Black)	4:00	1-act	My mama used to... (BPP 47)
DOES A TIGER WEAR A NECKTIE?—Don Petersen	Linda (18, Black)	3:00	I, 2	One day last winter...* (DPS 36)
THE FANTOD Amlin Gray	Rachel (15)	1:15	II, 2	The Spring is at... (DPS 40)
KID CHAMPION Thomas Babe	Alice (15)	1:00	sc. 10	You guys have been...* (DPS 59)
LAST LOOKS Grace McKeaney	Mercedes (14)	1:00	II, 2	You weren't at the club...* (DPS 65)
THE LATE CHRISTOPHER BEAN--Sidney Howard	Abby (19)	1:00	II	Oh, I remember! (SF 50)
MY SISTER IN THIS HOUSE—Wendy Kesselman	Lea (17)	1:45	I, 1	Dear Christine. When... (SF 8)
OUT OF GAS ON LOVERS LEAP—Mark St. Germain	Myst (17)	1:30	II	I was staying at...* (DPS 41)
THE RED COAT John Patrick Shanley	Mary (16)	1:00	1-act	Oh, that coat!* (DPS 11)
RITES Caroline White	Anne (18)	3:30	1-act	Hello. My name is Anne. (Dram 51)
YENTL Napolin & Singer	Anshel/Yentl (18, Jewish)	1:45	Prologue	Hello. My name is... (SF 7)

AGES 20 - 30

THE ADVERTISEMENT Natalia Ginzburg in "Plays By & About Women"	Teresa (20's)	3:45	I	I said to him... (RH 310)

ALL MEN ARE WHORES David Mamet in "Short Plays and Monologues"	Patti (20's)	1:45	sc. 9	I want to tie... (DPS 76)
BALM IN GILEAD Lanford Wilson	Darlene (22)	8:00	II	It's a kind of horse. (H&W 53)
BIRDBATH Leonard Melfi in "Encounters"	Velma (26)	1:30	1-act	Well, sometimes Mr. Quincy... (SF 14)
COMANCHE CAFE William Hauptman	Ronnie (20's)	1:45	1-act	There's a whole... (SF 12)
CRIMES OF THE HEART Beth Henley	Babe (24)	2:00	I	And we were just... (DPS 31)
CRIMES OF THE HEART Beth Henley	Meg (27, Southern)	2:00	III	Good morning.* (DPS 57)
THE DAYS AND NIGHTS OF BEEBEE FENSTER- MAKER—William Snyder	Beebee (20's, Southern)	4:00	III	"When where you are is where... (DPS 60)
FIVE ON THE BLACK HAND SIDE Charlie L. Russell	Gail (20, Black)	1:15	I, 1	Daddy is such a phony.* (SF 11)
GETTING OUT Marsha Norman	Arlie (20's)	2:15	I	So, there was... (DPS 9)
THE GOOD WOMAN OF SETZUAN Bertolt Brecht	Shen Te (20's)	1:00	sc. 4	How wonderful to see... (Grove 66)
I AM A CAMERA John Van Druten	Sally (20's)	1:00	III, 3	Well, there is a man.* (DPS 82)
KENNEDY'S CHILDREN Robert Patrick	Wanda (20's)	1:15	II	But there are... (SF 43)
LATER Corinne Jacker	Laurie (20's)	1:30	I, 2	To lie back... (DPS 35)
LAUNDRY & BOURBON James McLure	Elizabeth (20's, Texan)	1:15	1-act	I remember I was...* (DPS 16)
A MAP OF THE WORLD David Hare	Peggy (Early 20's)	1:30	I, 3	When I was sixteen... (SF 45)

THE MIGHTY GENTS Richard Wesley	Rita (28, Black)	3:00	sc. 5	I used to be... (DPS 19)
A MOON FOR THE MISBEGOTTEN Eugene O'Neill	Josie (28, Irish)	1:45	III	That's right. Do what... (SF 92)
PLAY MEMORY Joanna M. Glass	Jean (28, Canadian)	1:15	II	I am twelve now. (SF 52)
PLENTY David Hare	Susan (20's, English)	2:15	sc. 4	I want to move on.* (SF 27)
RAINDANCE M. Z. Ribalow	Falina (20's, Mexican)	1:15	I	Hello, all you... (SF 7)
THE ROOM—Harold Pinter in "Complete Works: One"	Mrs. Sands (20's, English)	1:45	1-act	Yes, Mrs. Hudd, you see... (Grove 116)
SAY GOODNIGHT, GRACIE--Ralph Pape	Catherine (Late 20's)	3:00	1-act	I was in high school...* (DPS 31)
THE SILVER CORD Sidney Howard	Christina (20's)	2:00	II, 1	Once last winter we... (SF 34)
STILL LIFE Emily Mann	Cheryl (28)	3:00	II, 4	Every day before... (DPS 42)
THE TIME OF YOUR LIFE William Saroyan	Kitty (20's)	1:00	I	I dream of home. (SF 42)
TWO SMALL BODIES Neal Bell	Eileen (Late 20's)	2:00	II, 1	I told them to... (DPS 27)
UNCOMMON WOMEN & OTHERS Wendy Wasserstein	Kate (27)	2:30	II, 6	Carter, do you... (DPS 44)
THE VALUE OF NAMES Jeffrey Sweet	Norma (22)	1:15	1-act	I was fifteen years... (DPS 15)
THE WARM PENINSULA Joe Masteroff	Ruth (20's)	2:00	I	They say all brides are... (SF 5)
THE WARM PENINSULA Joe Masteroff	Joanne (20's)	1:00	I	There are a couple of cities... (SF 6)

THE ART OF DINING Tina Howe	Elizabeth (Mid 30's)	1:15	II, 2	In fact, when... (SF 52)
THE BALCONY Jean Genet	Irma (30's)	1:00	sc. 5	The horde, but we have... (Grove 40)
A BEQUEST TO THE *NATION*—Terence Rattigan	Emma (30's, English)	1:30	II	But how do I see myself?* (Dram 87)
CANDIDA Bernard Shaw	Candida (33, English)	1:15	III	Now I want you to look... (Peng 73)
CHAPTER TWO Neil Simon	Jennie (32)	3:15	II, 7	You know what... (SF 119)
CLOUDS Michael Frayn	Mara (30's)	1:15	I, 5	The children have... (SFL 30)
COME BACK TO THE *5 & DIME, JIMMY DEAN,* *JIMMY DEAN* Ed Graczyk	Mona (30's, Texan)	1:45	II	That night, I laid there...* (SF 70)
COME NEXT TUESDAY Frank D. Gilroy in "Present Tense"	Wife (Late 30's)	6:00	1-act	The same when the...* (SF 37)
A DAY IN THE DEATH *OF JOE EGG* Peter Nichols	Pam (30's, English)	2:00	II	It wasn't my idea... (SF 44)
THE DINING ROOM A.R.Gurney, Jr.	Ruth (30's)	1:00	II	Lately, I've been... (DPS 69)
FATHER'S DAY Oliver Hailey	Marian (30's)	1:00	I	That's wonderful, Estelle. (DPS 22)
THE GOOD DOCTOR Neil Simon	Wife (30's)	2:00	I, 6	No! Not a word! (SF 45)
THE GREAT NEBULA *IN ORION*—Lanford Wilson	Louise (30's)	2:45	1-act	I know it must seem... (DPS 16)
IS THERE LIFE AFTER *HIGH SCHOOL?*--J. Kindley	Ginny (30's)	1:30	II	I like to think... (SF 36)

THE JUNIPER TREE Wendy Kesselman	Stepmother (30's)	2:30	sc. 2	GOD. After she died... (SF 17)
MARIE AND BRUCE Wallace Shawn	Marie (Early 30's)	4:00	1-act	I was tired. I was... (DPS 10)
NO TIME FOR COMEDY S.N. Behrman	Amanda (30)	2:30	II	Now just sit down...* (SF 53)
OLD TIMES—Harold Pinter in "Complete Works: Four"	Kate (30's, English)	2:30	II	But I remember you. (Grove 67)
ONCE MORE, WITH FEELING Harry Kurnitz	Dolly (30's)	1:30	III	What did Dr. Fabian do? (DPS 49)
OUT OF OUR FATHER'S HOUSE—Eve Merriam	Elizabeth (30's)	1:45	1-act	When I was... (SF 16)
OUT OF OUR FATHER'S HOUSE—Eve Merriam	Gertrude (30's)	1:15	1-act	My father did not... (SF 22)
PAINTING CHURCHES Tina Howe	Mags (Early 30's)	4:30	I, 3	I guess I was afraid...* (SF 50)
THE PRIME OF MISS JEAN BRODIE Jay Allen	Brodie (35, English)	2:15	II, 5	I will not resign... (SF 57)
SEA MARKS Gardner McKay	Timothea (30's, Welsh)	1:30	I, 5	And you are the...* (SF 39)
SNOW LEOPARDS Martin Jones	CJ (30's, West Virginian)	4:30	II	I did somethin' real... (SF 48)
THE VAMPIRES Harry Kondoleon	Pat (33)	1:30	I	C, are you awake? (DPS 6)
THE WISDOM OF EVE Mary Orr & Reginald Denham	Karen (30's)	2:45	I	Ladies and Gentlemen, I'm... (DPS 7)

AGES 40 - 60

AND THINGS THAT GO BUMP IN THE NIGHT Terrence Mc Nally	Ruby (50's)	1:15	II	I mean there you... (DPS 66)

Play / Author	Character	Time	Act/Scene	First line / Source
BOESMAN AND LENA Athol Fugard	Lena (50's, Black)	3:30	I	Let's have a... (SF 13)
A BREEZE FROM THE GULF—Mart Crowley	Loraine (40's)	2:00	I, 3	Daddy and I had...* (SF 21)
BROADWAY BOUND Neil Simon	Kate (50)	7:00	II	The night I danced...* (SF 82)
BRONTOSAURUS Lanford Wilson	Dealer (45)	4:30	1-act	But what does it... (DPS 17)
CLOUD NINE Caryl Churchill	Betty (Middle-aged, English)	1:30	II, 4	I used to think... (SF 95)
COMANCHE CAFE William Hauptman	Mattie (40's)	1:30	1-act	When we started...* (SF 10)
THE DARK IS LIGHT ENOUGH Christopher Fry	Countess (50)	1:30	II	Not as they are... (DPS 58)
DEAR LIAR Jerome Kilty	Mrs. Campbell (40's, English)	1:30	II	New York, August 1937... (SF 51)
THE EFFECT OF GAMMA RAYS ON MAN-IN-THE-MOON MARIGOLDS Paul Zindel	Beatrice (45)	3:00	I, 2	Science, science, science! (DPS 18)
THE FOURPOSTER Jan de Hartog	She (40's)	1:30	III, 1	I didn't intend to say... (SF 49)
THE GINGERBREAD LADY Neil Simon	Evy (40's)	1:30	I	You're seventeen years old...* (SF 28)
THE GOOD AND FAITHFUL SERVANT Joe Orton in "Complete Plays"	Mrs. Vealfoy (40's, English)	2:00	sc. 3	We all know why... (Grove 159)
THE GRASS HARP Truman Capote	Catherine (50, Black)	2:00	I, 1	I know the French...* (DPS 8)
LATER Corinne Jacker	Molly (50's)	2:30	I, 1	There's no privacy... (DPS 24)
MALCOLM Edward Albee	Madame Girard (Middle-aged)	1:30	II, 4-5	I understand—though one is never sure... (DPS 52)

THE MATCHMAKER Thornton Wilder	Mrs. Levi (Uncertain age)	2:30	IV	Ephraim Levi, I'm going to get married... (SF 109)
MORE STATELY *MANSIONS*—Eugene O'Neill	Deborah (45)	3:00	I, 1	What can you expect... (Yale 3)
THE MUTILATED Tennessee Williams	Celeste (50)	1:45	sc. 2	Hmm, I wonder... (DPS 43)
NAOMI COURT Michael Sawyer	Sally (40's)	2:15	I, 3	Oh, Lenny, this... (SF 21)
A NIGHT OUT Harold Pinter in "Complete Works: One"	Mother (50's, English)	3:30	II, 2	Albert! Albert! (Grove 231)
ON TIDY ENDINGS Harvey Fierstein in "Safe Sex"	Marion (40)	4:30	1-act	Arthur, you don't under- stand.* (Atheneum 98)
RED ROVER, RED ROVER Oliver Hailey	Vic (40's)	1:00	II	Standing in line... (DPS 37)
THE SILVER CORD Sidney Howard	Mrs. Phelps (50's)	1:45	I	Now you must try... (SF 19)
SMALL CRAFT *WARNINGS* Tennessee Williams	Leona (Middle-aged)	1:45	I	I told you privately... (ND 33)
TWIGS George Furth	Celia (50's)	3:00	I, 2	Phil and me moved...* (SF 30)

AGES 60 AND OVER

ALL OVER Edward Albee	Mistress (61)	2:30	II	I don't know. (SF 60)
HAROLD AND MAUDE Colin Higgins	Maude (80)	1:00	I, 12	Oh, yes. Look at...* (SF 56)
THE MAN WHO STAYED *BY HIS NEGATIVE* Peter Dee	Woman (Old)	2:15	1-act	Young man, are you alright? (SF 20)
THE WINSLOW BOY Terence Rattigan	Violet (Old, English)	1:15	II, 2	Oh, Miss Kate... (DPS 84)

ONE CHARACTER PLAYS

PLAY Author	Character (Age)	Time	Place	Edition, page
ANIMAL—Oliver Hailey in "Picture, Animal Crisscross"	The Woman (Middle-aged)	4:30	1-act	DPS 25
BAG LADY Jean-Claude Van Itallie	Clara (Early 50's)		Full-length	DPS
BEFORE BREAKFAST Eugene O'Neill in "Six Short Plays"	Mrs. Rowland (20's)	10:00	1-act	RH 4
THE BELLE OF AMHERST William Luce	Emily (53)		Full-length	Houghton Mifflin
AN EDUCATED LADY Ken Jenkins in "Rupert's Birthday..."	Lady (Any, Southern)		1-act	DPS 41
EMMA GOLDMAN: LOVE, ANARCHY & OTHER AFFAIRS—Jessica Litwak in "Women Heros"	Emma (30's)		1-act	Applause 40
HOW SHE PLAYED THE GAME—Cynthia L. Cooper in "Women Heroes"	Various		1-act	Applause 74
LAUGHS, ETC. James Leo Herlihy in "Stop, You're Killing Me"	Gloria (40)	12:00	1-act	DPS 7
LILLIAN William Luce	Lillian Hellman		Full-length	DPS
A LOVELY LIGHT Dorothy Stickney	Edna St. Vincent Millay (Middle-aged)		Full-length	SF
MAGGIE & PIERRE Linda Griffiths	Various		Full-length	Talonbooks

MILLIE Susan Kander in "Women Heroes"	Millie (45, Black)	1-act	Applause 92
MISS MARGARIDA'S *WAY* Roberto Athayde	Miss Margarida (Any)	Full- length	SF
ONE WOMAN SHOW Cornelia Otis Skinner	Various	Full- length	Dram
ORGASMO ADULTO *ESCAPES FROM THE ZOO* Franca Rame & Dario Fo	Various	Full- length	BPP
PERSONALITY Gina Wendkos & Ellen Ratner in "Women Heroes"	Lorette (30, Jewish)	1-act	Applause 26
ROSARY Jean-Claude Van Itallie in "7 Short & Very Short Plays"	Nun (20's)	1-act	DPS 33
RUPERT'S BIRTHDAY Ken Jenkins	Louisa (30's)	1-act	DPS 7
THE SEARCH FOR SIGNS *OF INTELLIGENT LIFE IN* *THE UNIVERSE* Jane Wagner	Various	Full- length	Harper & Row
TALKING WITH Jane Martin	Various	Full- length	SF
THURSDAY IS MY DAY *FOR CLEANING* Jordan Crittenden	Louise (33)	1-act	SF
ZELDA William Luce	Zelda Fitzgerald (47, Southern)	Full- length	SF